DON'T TELL I, TELL 'EE!

An affectionate look at the
Somerset dialect

Roger Evans

with illustrations by Richard Scollins
and Pat Frost

COUNTRYSIDE BOOKS
NEWBURY BERKSHIRE

First published 2005
© Roger Evans 2005

COUNTRYSIDE BOOKS
3 Catherine Road
Newbury Berkshire

To view our complete range of books,
please visit us at
www.countrysidebooks.co.uk

ISBN 1 85306 916 7
EAN 978185306 916 1

Designed by Peter Davies, Nautilus Design
Produced through MRM Associates Ltd, Reading
Printed by Arrowsmith, Bristol

CONTENTS

DON'T TELL I, TELL 'EE!

Both publisher and author acknowledge with gratitude the debt they owe to *Ey Up Mi Duck!* by Richard Scollins and John Titford, first published in 1976. That book was the inspiration for the series of regional dialect volumes of which this is one.

FOREWORD

*Whirr be gwain to? Tiz getting dimpsey, zo cummin yer an wet thee's
whistle. Yer, which o they jars is owern? Thiky ones yourn, inner?
Dang I if there ain't a gurt big wapse innun.*

These scraps of Somerset dialect could be a foreign tongue but they are the language of my youth, dialect that survives in the school playground, in the bars of village pubs and the homes of farming communities. Most of us, as we mature, lose our dialect – it is our way of dealing with a shrinking world. We hold telephone conversations with people hundreds of miles away and watch countless hours of 'well spoken' television. Our dialect fades. But I have never lost my love of genuine dialect and have the same passion for its discovery as I do for any foreign language.

But I do mean dialect – not English spoken with a funny accent, legitimised by adding lots of 'ooh-aars' and eventually making some reference to Zummerzet Zyder. Dialect contains its own vocabulary with words such as *dimpsey*, the Somerset expression for that half-light which comes at the end of the day, and *dumbledore* for bumblebee. I once watched an episode of the television programme *Call my Bluff* where unusual words are given three definitions by the members of one team whilst the members of the other try to guess which is correct. I couldn't believe it when no one guessed the answer for 'Dimpsey – A Somerset expression for the half-light at the end of the day – twilight'. I had grown up with the word in my vocabulary and had never realised it was so localised.

In the Somerset dialect,

Minehead Harbour

The George at Norton St Philip

we can find the remnants of Anglo-Saxon. The pronunciation is an ancient one where S is often, but not always, sounded as a Z; F sounds as a V and vowel sounds gain an R. It's the sounds and words of the court of King Alfred.

I remember when I took my GCE 'O' Level French oral examination. The examiner remarked that never before had he heard French spoken with such a strong Somerset accent. I wasn't sure if that was a compliment or a criticism. In later years whilst working in both France and Canada, with French speaking Canadians, I was fascinated to discover that my 'Somerset' French was better received in Canada. It perhaps reflected how so many West Country folk emigrated to North America in the centuries during which the dialect of the New World was evolving.

I commend the reader to experience the pleasures of well spoken Somerset dialect, especially by visiting some remote country inns, frequented by locals – just sit back and listen; the later it is in the evening, the stronger the dialect.

I acknowledge the help of Bob Willy, Annie and Graham Truman and the regulars at Bridgwater's Annie's Bar who never object when I whip out the note book to jot down another Somerset expression. And I pay homage to those students of the Somerset dialect who some hundred years ago documented its phonetics, scholars such as George Parker, Frederick Elworthy, Walter Raymond, W.H. Cooke (alias Tommy Nutty), William McMillan, George Sweetman and numerous other who have left us a rich legacy of dialect poems and stories from around the county. Also acknowledgement is given to Richard Scollins for his 'Almost Totally Insane Look at British History' pictures, and Pat Frost for her sketches.

Roger Evans

INTRODUCTION

The Somerset Dialect

Somerset is a large county and the dialect varies considerably. Saxon invaders came to England in clans, each with its own dialect, and the dialects heard today across the county mark the areas in which those clans settled. In Somerset, the Britons were driven westward but the River Parrett, which had formed a natural barrier between Celtic tribes, proved a hindrance to the advance of the Saxons. Hence in eastern and central Somerset the dialect is practically Anglo-Saxon. To the west of the Parrett, especially around the Brendon Hills and Exmoor, the dialect is spoken with a Celtic accent and closely resembles that of Devon. Many Celtic words survive, such as *bastick* (basket), *woh* (a command for a horse to stop), *fagot* (bundle of wood) and *mattock* (a cutting tool).

Thus we can understand how dialect in Somerset can vary as we travel the county. Apart from the East-West divide formed by the River Parrett, the area to the north of the Mendip Hills also has its own dialect. One notable example of this is in the way that words are sounded when they end in a vowel. A good *idea* in Bristol and its surrounding *area* become a good *ideal* in that *aerial*. In the rest of Somerset, they become *idee-yer* and *airier*. Hence Ls or Rs are added to the ends of words according to geographic location. Generally speaking, in Somerset dialect, it is the R sound that is the noticeable clue. Hence my wife's name, Lorna, is pronounced locally as Lorner, to which she is accustomed. But she cannot tolerate hearing her name collecting the North Somerset 'L'. When introduced to a Bristolian, she introduces herself simply as 'Lorn', dropping the trailing 'a'. It can also be unfortunate for ladies by the names of *Eva* and *Ida* who become *evil* and *idle*!

I have often observed how the Somerset dialect is disappearing and hence in this volume I have included a mixture of both older dialect, which can still be heard amongst the senior members of the remoter communities, and the newer Somerset dialect which is much softer than that of earlier generations. This mix of old and new can cause confusion. Whilst talking to some locals in a north Somerset pub, I picked up on a particularly strong dialect from a lady in the bar.

'Whirr be she vrom?' I asked my friend. 'Alasker,' came the reply. I knew there was no way this lady was from North America and was surprised at my friend's response. She was broad Somerset.

'She ain't niver vrom Alasker,' I protested. 'No,' said my friend, 'I 'ant ast 'er yet.' I then realised his *Alaska* was *I'll ask her*. He turned to the lady and enquired, 'Yer, skews I, but ifee doan mine I askin, which part of county be thee vrom?' to which she replied 'Banes'. He looked at me quizzically and said, 'She do talk bloody good Zummerzet vur a vorraner.' To this day he remains totally unaware of the new county administrative boundaries where BANES is Bath and North East Somerset.

Dialect continually evolves. In Somerset, the remnants of the language of King Alfred form just one part of our heritage. It is rich in vocabulary and pleasant to the ear, as the following pages hopefully demonstrate. English is the expressive language of poets because of that variety. Somerset dialect adds to that richness, not just with pronunciation, but with words not found further afield. If we lose that dialect, our language will lack the richness it has. It is important, therefore, to record and preserve this evolving part of our cultural heritage. Use it or lose it. Treat it like an endangered species or while you're not watching, the words will disappear forever.

CHAPTER 1

A Look at Nursery Rhymes

Jack and Jill (Pat Frost)

Various villages around the country will lay claim to being the origin of certain nursery rhymes. Jack and Jill is just one example and the Somerset village of Kilmersdon has a justifiable claim to its ownership. The rhyme dates back some 450 years and refers to the well at the top of Bad Stone Hill. The well survives to this day but was sealed up several decades ago when the local headmaster considered it a danger to the children. Jack and Jill were apparently unmarried lovers in the late 15th century.

> *Jack and Jill went up the hill*
> *To fetch a pail of water*
> *Jack fell down and broke his crown ...*

Jack it seems was killed by a boulder, which, perhaps through frost damage, broke free, tumbled down the hill and smashed his skull. Death was almost instantaneous. This possibly accounts for the name Bad Stone Hill! However, it definitely accounts for Jack's untimely death.

And Jill came tumbling after.

A few days later, Jill died in childbirth. This links in closely with the nursery rhyme. But how do we convince those from other villages around the country that this is truly a Somerset born story? Is there evidence that tips the balance Somerset's way?

Where else in the country is there a well at the top of hill, when gravity is inclined to take water downhill? Such hilltop water supplies are most unusual and will eliminate most of the other pretenders to the title. But where can we find even more incontrovertible evidence? It's easy – and brings us back to dialect. The answer lies in the rhyme. *Jill* and *hill* are rhyming words. *Down* and *crown* likewise rhyme but *water* and *after* do not. Now let's translate the poem into Somerset dialect.

> *Jack and Jill went up the hill*
> *To vetch a payul of wadder*
> *Jack fell down and broke he's crown*
> *An' Jill camed tumbling adder.*

It rhymes. I rest my case! A similar example comes in a bellringers' verse, collected by Ruth Tongue, who recorded so much of Somerset's folklore, in 1910:

> *Old John Wesley's dead and gone*
> *He left us in the tower;*
> *'Twas his desire that we should play*
> *At eight and twelve and fower.*

Notice how the rhyme only works if *four* is sounded in correct dialect as *fower*.

Not far from Kilmersdon can be found the village of Mells and its association with the *Little Jack Horner* rhyme is beyond doubt. During the reign of Henry VIII, when monasteries were being closed down, Richard Whiting, the Abbot of Glastonbury, presented a gift to the King to gain his favour. The gift was a pie that contained, within its crust, the title deeds to twelve manors. Jack Horner was the Abbot's trusted steward and was charged with delivering the pie. However, on his way he removed the deeds for the manor of Mells and after the dissolution took up residence there. His descendants continued to live there up until 1975.

Little Jack Horner sat in his corner
Eating his Christmas pie.
He put in his thumb and pulled out a plum
And said 'What a good boy am I.'

Mells was the plum that Jack Horner took out. Of course, his family always denied the allegation, claiming that he had actually paid £1,831 9s 3d for its purchase. They also point out that Thomas Horner and not Jack was the original owner of the manor. Can the story be true? Villains, irrespective of their true names, were often referred to as knaves or 'Jacks'. Is it likely that such valuable items as deeds would be carried in a pie? Quite possibly. The highways were not safe places and it was wise to disguise valuables by whatever means were available. Whether or not Jack Horner betrayed the abbot, we will never know but at least we can say with confidence that the associated nursery rhyme has its origins in the Somerset village of Mells.

CHAPTER 2

Somerset Grammar

Learning the Somerset dialect, like learning any language, requires a basic understanding of the verbs 'to be' and 'to have'. With the verb 'to be', there is a clear difference between old Somerset and modern Somerset dialect.

ENGLISH	OLD SOMERSET	MODERN SOMERSET
I AM	I BE	I IZ
YOU ARE	THEE BIST	YOU BE OR YOU IZ
HE IS	'E BIST	'E BE
IT IS	TIZ	TIZ
WE ARE	UZ BIST	WE BE OR WE IZ
THEY ARE	THEY BIST	THEY IZ OR THEY BE
I AM NOT	I BAINT	I 'AINT

Exmoor timber passing through Dunster

Perhaps the greatest confusion for those unfamiliar with the language comes from the way pronouns alter. *He* becomes *her*, *you* becomes *he* and *we* becomes *us*.

Ee'ze a good'n, inn'er.	He's a good one, isn't he.
Uz'ad bedder ask'n t'come along, do'ee dink zo?	We'd better ask him to come along – do you think so?

Other variations are:

In'I?	Am I not?
In'ee?	Are you not?
Inner?	Is he not?
Innuz?	Are we not?
Innum?	Are they not?
Waddun I?	Wasn't I?
Tid'n or tint	It isn't
Ad I abin	Had I been
Ad I azeen	Had I seen
I 'ave	I have
'Ee az	He has
Ur az	She has
Ant, eg I ant, you ant, they ant	Have not
Ann-eye?	Have I not?
Ann-ee?	Have you not?
Ann-she?	Has she not?
Ann-ur?	Has he not?
Ann-uz?	Have we not?
Annum?	Have they not?

The next lesson comes with an understanding of the transposition of letters, the commonest of which is the letter 'r'. In Saxon words, the 'r' and the vowel sound are often swapped over. Thus *great* becomes *gurt*, *run* becomes *urn*, *children* becomes *chillurn* and *rudduck* becomes *urdock*, as in *Robin Urdock* for *Robin Redbreast*. Surviving examples can be seen in the expression 'Hurdy Gurdy Man'. The Hurdy Gurdy Man is someone with an old stringed instrument that is played by turning a handle at one end. The player's face was traditionally made red, or ruddied. Hence *Ruddy* becomes *Hurdy*.

'The people I have cared for most, and who have seemed most worth caring for ... have been very simple folk.' (J.M. Barrie)

Iz they thur yur chillurn?	Are those your children?

In similar fashion, the letter 's' will often be transposed:

Wapse	Wasp
Ax	Ask
Apse	Asp

An 'a' when added to the front of a verb puts it into the past tense:

If I'd I a-knowed, I ooden a-went.	I wouldn't have gone if I'd known.
They bin agone vur aah-vower be now.	They've been gone for half an hour now.
Az'n thee bin aplowun zmarnin?	Haven't you been ploughing this morning?
An'ee abin adder'n?	Haven't you been after him?

A 'y' may be added to the end of words to turn nouns into verbs:

I be gwain milky and then adder that I d'thatchy 'til it d'get dimpsey.	I am going milking and after that I'll do some thatching until it starts to get dark.

The 'th' sound is almost always hard. According to which part of the county is concerned, the hardness may at its minimum simply be formed by pressing the tongue more firmly against the upper front teeth than would be the norm, and could be expressed as 'dh', but in its hardest form 'th' becomes a 'd' sound. Three becomes dree, *thread* becomes *dread*, and *through* becomes *droo*.

Further variations on this theme come with prepositions such as *this*, *that*, *these* and *those* where additional words are added to provide emphasis:

Thiky'un thur, urz bigger'n tuther.	That one there is bigger than the other.
Thikeeze ever z'much worser'n tuther.	That is ever so much worse than the other.
Theeze yur	These here
Thay thur	Those there
Av-ee zeed thik ther knife o'mine?	Have you seen my knife?

CHAPTER 3

Getting By in Somerset

Alasker	I'll ask her
Art noon	Good afternoon
Awe rye den?	All right, then?
Bide thur awhile, willey?	Wait there, please
Come inyer and wet thee whizzle	Come in here and have a drink
Ease a guddun, inner?	He's a good one, isn't he?
Gid out wi'ee	Go on with you
Gitten dimpsey	Becoming dark (*dimpsey* is the half-light period after sunset: still enough light to find your way but only just enough to read by)
Goin' down the garden	Going to the toilet
I mind th'owed dayz	I remember the old days
Le' 'er ('un) bide	Leave her (him) alone
Marnin	Good morning
Ouzes thisisis?	To whom does this belong?

Ouze yer ma'e?	Who's your friend?
Ow beyon, m'deeyurs?	How are you, my friends?
Prapper job	Genuine article; task well completed
Prapper vair weather	In Bridgwater this means a deluge of rain (referring to the perception that it always rains for the four days of Bridgwater Fair); elsewhere means fine weather
Righ'?	Hello, are you all right?
Thiky ones yourn, inner?	That one's yours, isn't he?
'Ungry azzun 'unter	As hungry as a horse
Up tuther zide-a feeyuld	The far side of the field
Uz dunno	We don't know
Wassee zayin?	What are you saying?
Wasser doin'?	What's he doing?
Wasson den?	What's on, then?
Wha' be bout then?	What are you doing?
Whirr beeyee?	Where are you?
Whirr be gwain to?	Where are you going?
Whirr be she?	Where is she?
Whirr she vrom? Alasker	Where is she from? I'll ask her
Whirr she vrom? Alasker	Where is she from? Alaska
Whirr zee to?	Where are you?
Whirr zur to?	Where is he?
Whirr beeyum?	Where are they?
Why doanee look wur you'm gwain?	Why don't you look where you're going?
Wossup?	What's happening?
Wossup to?	What are you doing?

Awe rye den? is the most common greeting to be used in Somerset dialect. It means 'All right, then?' and in its literal senses is an enquiry after one's state of health. However, the response should be *Awe rye* and not 'Yes, thank you.' It will commonly be abbreviated to just *Rye?* As a greeting, it is even used in the most casual of meetings, perhaps with a stranger on a footpath. *Ow beyon?* is another greeting but this is inappropriate for use with a stranger. It is more correct when encountering a previous acquaintance. On departing, *Z'long, zee yer* is expressed and means 'So long. I'll see you again.' However, this also is used even when leaving someone never likely to be seen again.

CHAPTER 4

A Somerset Dictionary

AThe greater majority of the words below are in common use today. Many, however, may only be heard in isolated parts of Somerset and some are no longer in modern day usage. The problem is that it's a bit like watching endangered species. Just when you believe that the last of the line has disappeared, someone reports a sighting in a remote spot somewhere. It's the same with dialect but the absence of some of the following words in modern Somerset dialect helps to emphasise what we stand to lose.

Aah and **aarr**, eg **well aah**	Yes
Acker	Friend
Adder	After
Addle	A pus filled swelling
Addled	Gone off, as in a bad egg
Again	Against
Agen	Again
Aggy	Gather eggs, eg *I be gwain aggy*
Agin	Against
Agon	Gone
Aiyer	Air
Alasadaizey	Alackaday, alas
Ale	A weak beer, generally meaning it has fewer than five bushels of malt per hogshead
Alice	Ulcer
Allus	Always
Anigh, anear	Near by
'Ankicher	Handkerchief
'Ammered	Drunk
Amper	Pimple
Ann Summer	More handsome
Anyhroad	Anyway

Anywhen	Any time
Apiggy back	Carried on shoulders, as for a child
Appleplexus	Apoplexy
Apricock	Apricot
Apse	Abscess
Apse	Hasp, fasten
Apsen	Made from the wood of the aspen tree
Arg, argify	Argue
Art'noon	Afternoon
Ass backards	Back to front

Minehead, The Sands and North Hill.

Ast	Asked
Astooded	Sunk into the ground
Athirt	Across
Auver	Over
Aveard	Afraid
Avord	Afford
Avore	Before
Awakid	Awake

Awmos'	Almost
Awrigh'	All right
Ax	Ask
Ayeard	Heard
Back house	Outhouse
Backalong	Some time ago
Bade	Bed
Bailly	Bailiff
Baint	Is not
Ballyrag	To scold, tell off especially with foul language
Bandy legs	Crooked legs
Batch	Hillock
Baven	Faggot of unprepared twigs and branches
Becall	Tell off
Bedstick	Stick used for bed turning, especially feather beds
Beer	A woodland suitable for feeding pigs on acorns and beechnuts
Beesom, besom	Broom made of twigs
Begrumpled	Offended
Begurge	Begrudge
Beknown	Known about
Benapt	Left high and dry by the tide
Bestest	Best
Betwaddled	Confused
Bibber	Shiver
Bibbler	A drinker
Biddle	Beetle
Bide	Stay
Biden	Staying
Bin	Been
Birchen	Made of birch wood
Bisghee	Axe for removing tree roots
Bissen	Are not
Bist	Are
Bit and drap	Meal
Blather	Fuss, uproar
Blind Buck and Davy	Blind Man's Buff

Blooth	Blossom
Bobbish	In full health and high spirits
Bog baler	Long handled scoop for emptying outdoor toilets
Bog house	Toilet

The outdoor toilet.

Bone shave	Sciatica
Bore	Tidal wave, especially on the Severn and Parrett rivers
Borrid	A sow ready to receive the boar
'Bout	About
Bow	Small arched bridge
Brassen	Made of brass
Breze	Press down
Brickle	Brittle
Brown kitties, brown titus	Bronchitis
Bruckly	Brittle, crumbly, falls apart easily

Bucket and chuck it	The outdoor toilet
Bull-beggar	Hobgoblin
Bundle along	Bound rapidly
Buppo, bup-horse	Stick with a horse's head handle
Bwile	To boil
By me by	By and by
Cack handed	Left handed
Caddle	Confusion, muddle
Cancervells	Icicles
Cannee?	Can you?
Cardin	According
Cassen	Cannot
Cassen thee?	Can you not?
Catcheldy	Changeable, indecisive
Chammer	Chamber
Chayer	Chair
Chimbley	Chimney
Chittlens	Pig's intestines
Chockful	Absolutely full
Chuffed	Pleased
Cider ring	Cider press
Cidered up	Drunk
Circoo	Circle
Claggy	Lumpy, muddy, as in heavy clay
Clapse	Clasp
Clavel	Fireplace beam
Clavel-tack, clavey-tack	Shelf over a fireplace beam, a mantelpiece
Cleeve	Steep slope
Clim, climmer	Climb
Cloam	Pottery
Clyce	River or land drain outlet controlled by a valve to let water out but not in
Cob	Mud and straw mix used to build house walls
Combe	Pronounced 'coom', a deep hollow valley
Comferbull	Comfortable
Cow-baby	Coward
Cradlehood	Infancy
Cre-apped	Crept

Creem	Sudden shiver
Crips	Crisp (as in sharp)
Crock	Metal cooking pot
Croopy down	Squat down
Crousty	Ill tempered
Cubby hole	Small cupboard
Cursmas	Christmas
Cuz	Because
Dabster	Expert
Dadder	Confuse
Dang I!	Well, I'll be damned!
Dank	Damp and dark
Dap	Bound along
Daps	Trainers
Darter	Daughter
Daver	Wilt, fall over
Deb'n	Devon
Desperd	Desperate
Dewbit	Breakfast
Dibs	Money
Diddee?	Did you?
Didden	Did not
Diddiky	Rotten, crumbling
Dimmet	The period of dusk after sunset
Dimpsey	Half-lit, at twilight or dusk
	Can also be used to describe partial sight
	or short sightedness
Din I?	Didn't I?
Dinner?	Didn't he?
Dinnum?	Didn't they?
Dinnuz?	Didn't we?
Dirn	Upright post supporting a doorway
Dish o' tay	Cup of tea
Dollop	Large lump
Donnins	Clothes
Dough baked	Simple (as in 'e be dough baked)
Dough boys	Dumplings
Downarg	To put down by argument
Draffit	Vessel in which to collect pig swill

Drang	Alleyway
Drash, drasher	Thresh, thresher
Drashel	Threshold
Drauve	Drove, a track between fields
Drawed	Drawn
Drawt	Throat
Dreckley	Soon
Dree	Three
Dre'un	Threaten
Dring, dringet	To gather as a crowd, a crowd
Drong	Narrow passageway
Drode	Threw
Droo	Through
Droe	Throw
Drub	Beat, drum out
Drubbin	Thrashing, beating

Burnham Donkeys

Ducks and Drakes, Ducks and Mallards	Game of skimming stones over the surface of water
Dudder	Deafen or confuse with loud noise
Dun	Brown
Dungery	Toilet
Durnt	Dare not
Easement	Relief
Edification	Education
'Ee	You
'Ees	Yes
Eezelf	Himself
Eller	Mischievous child (as in *a righ' little eller*)
Elmen	Made from elm
Emmets	Tourists in large numbers
Empt	To empty out
Er	Him or it
Eyesore	I saw
Fair t'middlin	So so
Fairy rade	Procession of fairies
Farty	Forty
Figgety puddin'	Plum pudding
Finnikee	Fussy
Firnd	Friend
Fi-yul	File (of soldiers but not the tool)
Frump	Trump up, falsify
Fuddled	Confused
Gad	Whipping stick, for horse riding, or a stake
Gaffer	Old man
Gallivantin	Straying from home
Gallox	Gallows
Gally	Frighten
Gallybeggar	Bugbear, hobgoblin
Garn	Garden
Gate shord	Place for a gate
Gawk	Gape, stare
Ghostisiz	Ghosts
Gi'	Give
Gi'd	Gave
Gimmaces	Chains in which a prisoner is hung

DON'T TELL I, TELL 'EE!

Girnin	Grinning
Gob	Mouth
Goozegogs	Gooseberries
Gore	Triangular piece of land
Gramfer	Grandfather
Grammer	Grandmother
Grockle	Tourist
Grockle shells	Caravans
Gruff, gruffer	Mine, miner
Gulch	Swallow fast
Gullivers	Masked men wearing tall hats and bedecked in ribbons (akin to Morris Dancers) who travel with the Hobby Horse in May Day celebrations, collecting money from passers by
Gurt, girt	Great
Gurt big dollop	Large lump
Gwain	Going
Gwains on	Affairs, unacceptable behaviour
Gwon	Gone
Haaf	Half
Hag-rod	Bewitched
Hang gallis	Fit for hanging, villainous
Hangles	Fire crook, a hanging rod with teeth at intervals from which a cooking pot can be hung at different heights
Haps	Fasten
Hard Cheddar	Bad luck
Hassen	Haven't
Hassen thee?	Haven't you?
Hele, hell	To pour
Hele tap	Residue left after pouring
Hellier	Roof tiler
Here away	Hereabouts
Hick	Hop on one leg
Hirches	Riches
Hizzen	His own
Hobblers	Men who haul and moor boats by rope
Hold wi'	Agree with

26

Holler	A hollow
Hollerday	Holiday
Holman	Made of holm oak
Hoppy cough	Whooping cough
Hornen	Made of horn
Hullerburrloo	A noisy confusion
Hulve	Turn or tip over
Hunky punks	Will-o-the-wisps, the souls of unbaptised children
Hurdy 'ead	Red head
Idden	Isn't
Influrmayshun	Inflammation
Inner? Inshee?	Isn't he? Isn't she?
Jack-o-lanterns	Will-o-the-wisps, the souls of unbaptised children
Jaunders	The jaundice
Jis	Just
Kecker	Windpipe
Keep	Large basket
Keeve	Large vessel used in brewing
Kirsen	Christen
Kirsmas	Christmas
Kittle smock	Smock frock
Lamb's wool	Mulled ale with spiced apple
Lameger	Crippled
Lants	Sand eels
Larn	Teach
Lart	Wooden flooring
Leastways	Anyhow
Leat	Water channel to supply a mill
Leb'm	Eleven
Lew	Sheltered from the wind
Lights	Lungs
Lookzee, lookeezee	Pay attention
Lookzo	So it appears
Lug	Long heavy pole
Maister	Mister
Maized	Mad, insane
Manchit, Manchip	Jam-filled rolled pastry, almost unique to Bridgwater

Mang	Mix
Marnen	Morning
Meach	Play truant from school
Mell	Meddle
Mid	Might (verb)
Midlen	Fairly well
Miff	Cause offence
Mind	Remember (eg *I d'mind my childhood*)
Minded	Inclined
Mommets	Effigies
Mote	Small piece
Mucker, ole mucker	Friend, friend of long standing
Mud horse	A type of sled with a ski-shaped base and wicker basket, used on the Somerset coast for fishing
Mugglin	Struggling
Mumper	Beggar
Mussen	Must not
Nappy	Uneasy
Natch	Natural dry cider
Natomy	Anatomy, skeleton
Nestle tripe	Runt, especially of pigs but also of a brood of chicks or nestlings
Nipper	Small boy
Nippy	Sharp
Noggerhead	Idiot
North eye	Squint eyed
Nosebag	Nosey parker
Nottled, nottlin'	Really cold
Nottlins, nettlins	Intestines (tied in knots and boiled for eating) of pigs or calves
Nummet, nammet	Bite to eat at lunchtime
Odds	Consequences (as in w*ha' odds izzit to I?* – of what consequence is it to me?)
'Ood	Would
'Ooden	Would not
Ope	Opening
Ourn	Ours
Overlook	Bewitch

Ower	Our
Pantiles	Roof tiles
Parget	Plaster the inside of a chimney with cowdung and lime mix
Passen	Parson
Peart	Lively
Peer	Appear
Pelm, pellum	Dust (NB 'pelmet', which keeps the dust off curtains)
Pew moanier	Pneumonia
Piller	Pillow
Pins, the	Cataracts
Pitch	To settle, particularly when referring to snow
Pixie led	Simple minded, crazed
Plim	Swell
Pole	Nape of the neck (NB 'pole-axed')
Privy	Outdoor toilet
Privy ladle	Long handled scoop to empty the privy
Puggle 'eaded	Drunk, stupid Cider drinkers can often be recognised by their rosy faces and inability to articulate – they are then considered puggle 'eaded
Punkies	Will-o-the-wisps, the souls of unbaptised children
Purdy	Pretty
Rafty	Rancid
Rampin	Raving mad
Ramshackle	Rickety
Rawd	Rode
Ray	To dress
Ream	Widen out
Revel	A wake
Rig	Struggle with walking
Rise	Raise
Rumatics	Rheumatism
Quag	Quagmire
Quarter aled	Paralysed
Quirky	Argumentative

Scollared	Taught
Scrammed	Shivering with cold
Scrape	Dripping, animal fat when spread on bread
Screws	Rheumatism
Scud	Scab
Sexton's bones	Rheumatism
Shard	Slither of wood or metal
Shatt'n	Shall not
Shower	Sure
Skag	Catch in such a way as to tear
Skimmerton	A ride on horseback as a form of ridicule or punishment
Small beer	A weak beer, fewer than five bushels of malt per hogshead
Smeech	Smoky smelling
Smitch	Dust cloud
Sno	You know
'Spec	Expect
'Spoase	Suppose
Spunkies	Will-o-the-wisps, the souls of unbaptised children
Starn	Starving
'Stead	Instead
Stummick	Stomach
Swaller	Swallow
Tacklacky	Footman who runs alongside his master
Taiters	Potatoes
Tamp	Pat down soil
Tetchy	Irritable
Tharns	Thorns
Thees	You
Theezelf	Yourself
Thik	That
Thiky one	That one
Thunder box	Toilet
Thur	There
Tidden	It isn't
Tiddivale	Decorate
Tooked	Taken

T'other	The other
Traipse	To tramp around
Trow	Sailing barge designed for use on the Severn and Parrett rivers
Truckle	A circular piece of wood or metal placed under an object in order to lift and carry it
Turbul	Terrible
Tuther	The other
Tuttey	Small bunch of flowers, posy
Twer, t'whirr	It was
T'whirrdun	It was not
Twoant	It won't
'Twoodden	It would not
Um	Them, they
Un	One (as in *'ees a good'un, in'ur?* – he is a good one, isn't he?)
Unket	Uncanny
Unray	Undress
Ups and goes	Arises and moves on
Ur	He, it
'Urdy	Ruddy
Urn	Run
Ut	It
Vadder	Father
Var	For (as in *whadee do tha' var?* – what did you do that for?)
Vardin	Farthing
Var'n, vor'n	For him
Vast	Fast
Vayer	Fair, as in a market or funfair but not as in fair play, which remains as 'fair'
Verkin	Firkin, a stone cider carrying jar
Vine	Fine or find
Vitten	Fitting
Vive	Five
Viyur	Fire
Vlood	Flood
Voaks	Folk
Volly	Follow

Vool	Fool
Vor	For
Vorgit	Forget
Vower	Four
Vright'n	Frighten
Vug	Blow with the elbow
Vurdur	Further
Vurdurmost	Furthest
Vurgot	Forgot
Vust	First
Vy-yul	File (tool)
Walkin' out	Courting
Wapse	Wasp
Warshin	Washing
Werden	Were not
Wetshod	Wet footed
Whirr	Where
Whitpot	Bread pudding
Whiver	Hover
Withy	Willow
Wuss	Worse
Yeow	Ewe
Yer	Here
Yer	Your
Yer tiz	Here it is
Yer uz be	Here we are
Yorn	Yours
Zackly	Exactly
Zeben	Seven
Zed	Said
Zez	Says
Zich	Such
Zim	Seem
Zix	Six
Zmarnin	This morning
Zummat	Something
Zummerzet	Somerset
Zyve	Scythe

CHAPTER 5

Pub Talk– The Harvest Home Supper

Twer tother end of laz Zeptember and zquire 'ad organized 'arvest 'oame zupper. He liked eeze bit o' vun, did the zquire and 'ee 'ood choose for ee jus' who eed be gwain to dance with. 'E 'ad a wickud zense of 'umour did the zquire.

Now iffen thee 'ad worked 'ard for 'un, ee'd match 'ee up with one of they purty girls. But iffen thee 'ad bin a lazy zod, then ee'd get eeze own back and match 'ee up with one of they lasses that you ooden normally pick be choice.

Well, Harry May, 'ee were given a good'n. Zquire zays to 'un, 'You've worked real 'ard, 'Arry, and you d'deserve to be gwain 'ome with a real purty girl on yer arm,' and 'ee introduced 'un like to Emmer. She were plain but zort a purty all the zame. 'Arry went away real chuffed like, wiv a gurt zmile on eeze faze.

The haymaking party

After an 'ard daze work (courtesy of Glastonbury Rural Life Museum)

Then zquire 'ee did come to Tommy Packer. Well, I'd awatched Tommy and 'ee were a gurt lazy zod. Niver did 'ard daze work ineeze life. An 'ee were ugly as zin wi a faze like a zack of chittlens. Twer only laz week when 'ee wer spozed tur be clearing they ewes out'a orchid, when he dezides to go scrumpin instead. Well, he were up a tree in th'orchard, an' the gurt daft lummox climbed out on a branch which weren't nowhirr near big nuff for'un. Branch snapped an 'ee valls down into brimbles an crashes droo 'um and ends up in zix voot reen an all covered in mud, 'ee were. Rabbuts woz runnin all auver place. Well, 'ee were in a real purdickeemunt and 'ee az to fine eeze way out droo a gurt thick 'edge of brimbles.

'Yer, come an git I ow' a yer,' he hollerz. Well, I coon't git down droo they brimbles to git to 'un zo I az to vine anudder way. Now Tommy 'ad lef ladder up against the tree in orchet an I figurze if I kin git thick ther ladder auver top of 'edge, praps I kin drag'n out. But 'eeze a gurt big zod and twood take more'n I to pull'n droo. Zo I gets the 'oss and tize the ladder to'un and then I zlings the ladder auver the brimbles. 'Yer tiz,' I yelled out. Course, 'edge were zo tall, twer bout zix foot 'igh. 'Ee coon't zee thik ladder acomin and now eeze got a gurt lump up eeze 'ead wur thik ladder introduced eezelf.

'Waddee do that var?' he shouts at I and I replize, 'Do'ee want my 'elp ur not?' Well, 'ee climbz up on ladder and an I do git the 'oss to start apullin. Zo, thur's Tommy, lyin' out 'long ladder like one o' dey patients on a stretcher, and faze down into brimbles. The old 'oss she do pull forards and drags Tommy droo thee 'edge. 'E were hollerin summut turble. 'You gurt okkard cuss', he shouts at I and I were only doin' me best.

Well, az 'e getz to top of the 'edge, the ladder, zted of pointing up like, 'e do start to point downards and top of ladder venchally starts to dig into the brimbles and gits ztuck. The old 'oss az to pull'n even 'arder like an venchally the brimbles do give way an Tommy, he da shoot forrards like a rocket an lanz 'ead vurst in a gurt big cow pat. 'E looked uz bad uz 'ee did zmell and 'ee were in a voul mood.

Adder ee'd cleared the muck away vrom eeze eyes wiv eeze 'ankicher, 'e wen' on 'ome to 'eeze mudders an she told I, she zed, 'I 'ad to warsh thik gurt lummox vrom 'ead to voot. 'E ztunk and 'e 'ad thorns in placees were they thorns dint never ought t'go.' Er reckon az 'ee coon't zit down vur bedder par' uv a week. Coon't zit down vur dinner, 'ee 'ad to croopy down like.

Anyhroads, back to 'arvest zupper and the zquire. There were Tommy covered in scratcheeze and ztill not zmellin' right. Zo I were gobsmacked when zquire sayze, 'Tommy, thee shall danze will thik thur Zally.' Now Zally were purtiest maid in village and I did vanzy 'er like mad. I were real disappointed like when I ayeard 'er name linked with Tommy's. Trouble now waz I weren't zure who were left and I aveard 'e might jist match I up wiv Ider coz she were only one I could remember.

Then it comed my turn and zquire says az to 'ow I kin partner up wi' Ider. Cooden abin worser. Now, I ain't got nuffink agin Ider, az zuch. Tiz jus dat, well, er'z awright with 'osses, and er kin 'andle a plough az good az any man, but er aint the purtiest girl in the village.

Now I ain't niver yeard no one challenge the zquire but I felt thur mus'ave bin zome kind o' mistek. 'Zquire,' sez I, 'Zquire, ow come adder I've aworked real 'ard vur'ee an niver missed a daze work an' niver once turned up az much az a minute late, zept vur marnin adder Burgewater Vair, and you d'pair I up wiv Ider. And Tommy, ooze the laziest zod on the varm, and ztill dunt know one end of pitchvork from tother, and ztill stinking like the back end of a cow barn, he da git Zally, purtiest girl in the village?'

Zquire looks I straight in faze, iver zo zerious like, an sez to I, 'Listen, you gurt vool, thee knaws as well az I, thee were late on the day adder Burgewater Vair, and atop of dat, Ider were the only one lef. Zo you git on with your puneeshmunt and let Zally git on wid'urz!'

CHAPTER 6

A Rural Glossary

Abbey	Great white poplar
Aish	Ash
Aller	Alder
Apple dore	Apple tree
Aps	Aspen tree
Archet	Orchard
Asker	Lizard
Bannut	Walnut
Barrow pig	Castrated pig
Barton	Farmyard
Bauker stone	Whetstone (sandstone) for sharpening scythes
Beady eyes	Pansy
Beasts	Cattle
Bee butt	Beehive
Bell flower	Daffodil
Belsh	Cut the dung away from around a sheep's tail
Billy	Bundle of wheat straw
Binnuck	Minnow
Bird battin'	Trapping birds at night with lamps and nets
Blether	Bleat
Blood sucker	Leech
Bloody warrior	Wallflower
Bovate	15 acres
Bran	Tree stump or lump of wood fit only for burning
Brimbles	Brambles, blackberries
Brock (animal)	Badger

Brock (peat)	Irregular shaped piece of turf
Broom squires	Quantock gipsies
Buddle	Corn marigold
Bullen	Wanting the bull
Burgett	Small enclosure
But	A conical, funnel shaped basket made from willow, used to trap salmon especially on the Parrett and Severn rivers
Butter and eggs	Narcissus
Callyvan	Pyramid shaped bird trap
Carn	Corn
Caruca	An eight oxen plough team
Carucate	The land that can be maintained by one plough team of oxen, typically 80 to 120 acres
Chick a beady	Chicks
Chilver	Ewe lamb
Chipples	Spring onions
Chuggy pegs	Woodlice
Clackers	Rattling bird scarer
Claps	Clasp
Cleve pink	A species of carnation that grows in Cheddar Gorge
Clever	Clover
Clider	Goose grass
Clote	Yellow waterlily
Cockygee	Sharp apple
Colley	Blackbird

Conies	Rabbits
Conygre, conergre	Rabbit warren
Cowlease	Unmown meadow
Crane	Heron
Craws	Crows
Cuckold	Burdock
Culver	Wood pigeon
Cutty wren	Wren
Diddikies	Gipsies
Dirsh	Thrush
Dishwasher	Pied wagtail
Dock	Crupper – a strap that passes from a saddle under a horse's tail
Dowser	Water diviner
Drang	Narrow enclosed lane
Dumbledore, drumbledrone	Bumblebee
Dunnock	Hedge sparrow
Eft, effet	Newt
Ellum	Elm
Elver	Young eel
Elverin'	Netting of elvers along river banks, especially beside the Parrett
Emmet batch	Ant hill
Emmets	Ants – or tourists in large numbers
Evet	Lizard
Fitch	Polecat or ferret
Flittermouse	Bat (flying variety)
Flushed	Fledged, left the nest
French nut	Walnut
Furze, fuzz	Gorse
Gale	Castrated bull
Gallitrap	Fairy ring
Ganny cock	Turkey cock
Ganny cock's knob	Red hanging appendage beneath a turkey's beak
Gil'cup	Buttercup
Glattin'	The practice of hunting and trapping conger eels with dogs

(Pat Frost)

DON'T TELL I, TELL 'EE!

Gold	Wild myrtle, sweet willow
Gookoo	Cuckoo
Hain	Leave a meadow ungrazed to allow cutting later
Hallantide	All Saints' Day, ie after Hallowe'en
Ham	Rich pasture
Hame	Pieces of wood or metal used to attach a horse's harness to the shafts
Hay maidens	Ground ivy
Haymakey	Haymaking
Helm	Wheat straw prepared for thatching
Hog	One year old sheep
Hoke	Gore, wound with horns
Hoop	Bullfinch
Horse stinger	Dragonfly
Hoss	Horse

Glatting on Kilve Beach (Michael Stirling)

Houzen	Houses
Hully	Long wicker trap for catching eels
Humdrum	Three wheeled horse-drawn cart
Jack-in-the-hedge	Wild garlic or garlic mustard
Jally-Vish	Jellyfish
Jenny	Wren
Keep	Cattle food
Keffel	Clapped out horse
Kex	Dried stalks of plants such as hemlock, a form in which it is especially poisonous to horses
Ladies' smock	Bindweed, convolvulus
Lady cow	Ladybird
Lampin'	Poaching deer by night, using large lights to shine in the eyes of the deer
Larks' leers	Arable land left idle
Laver	Yellow flag or iris
Lease	Glean after the reapers
Leathern mouse	Bat
Leaze	Field grazed through the summer
Lenny cocks	Daffodils
Lighting stock	Block to help in mounting a horse
Limbers	Shafts of a cart
Ling	Heather
Linny	Shed or outhouse attached to a barn or building
Lock	Small quantity of hay or straw
Lynch	A hillside field in which ploughing along the contours has turned the clods downhill to create a terrace
Marten	Barren heifer
May	Hawthorn blossom
Milky	To milk (as in *I be gwain milky* – I'm going milking)
Mixen	Dung heap
Moggie	Moorhen
Mommet	Scarecrow
Moor coot	Moorhen
Moors	Tree roots
Mouse snap	Mouse trap
Muggets	Calf or sheep intestines
Mump	Block of peat dug out by hand

DON'T TELL I, TELL 'EE!

Nap	Hillock
Nestle tripe	Runt, especially of pigs but also of a brood of chicks or nestlings
Nirrup	Donkey
Nist	Near
Oak web, woak web	Cockchafer
Orts	Remnants of fodder
Oxgang	Fifteen acres
Peewit	Lapwing

Peewit

Perry	Pear tree
Pick	Pitchfork
Pigs' hales	Haws, fruit of the hawthorn
Pig's looze	Pigsty
Pill coal	Peat dug from beneath a layer of clay
Pink	Chaffinch
Pook	Cones of wheat
Pray	Gather cattle into one herd
Pull reed	Long reeds grown in ditches, used in making ceilings
Putt	Two-wheeled tip cart
Rames	Dead stalks of potatoes
Rayballing	Catching eels using worms threaded onto worsted twine
Reed	Wheat straw for thatching
Reen	Rhyne, a deep man-made ditch used to drain the moors

Robin 'urdick	Robin
Ruckle, ruttle	Stack of peat
Ruddock	Robin
Scrape	Shallow watering hole scraped out to catch water for wild ponies and sheep
Screech owl	Tawny owl
Sea crow	Cormorant
Sharp	Wagon shaft
Shord	Gap in a hedge
Shute	Field running downhill
Skeer devil	Swift
Slait, sleights	Ground to which sheep are accustomed or generally a familiar area
Snags	Sloe berries on the small side
Snarley horns	Snails
Sour dock	Sorrel
Souse	Pig's ears
Spadger	House sparrow

Rayballing on the Somerset Levels (Michael Stirling)

Stacking peat

Spar	Willow rod used for fixing thatch to roofs
Spar gads	Sticks to be split into two
Spit	Dig with a spade, the distance covered in turning the spade
Spitter	Long handled tool for cutting weeds
Spuddlin'	Action of chickens scratching around in the soil; can also be used to refer to children playing in the dirt
Staddle	Framework forming the base for a hayrick
Stake hang	A circular fence of stakes driven in on the seashore to trap fish
Steart, stert	A narrow peninsula or a narrow strip of land between two stretches of water
Stitch	Ten sheaves of corn stacked together, alternatively a stand of rifles arranged in wigwam fashion
Stormcock	Mistle thrush
Stritch	Piece of wood used to scrape off surplus when corn is being measured

Stumpy	Wren
Swipe	Beat down bracken with rotating flails from the back of a tractor
Taiters or teddies	Potatoes
Tate	A hollow ruckle
Turd boxing	Muck spreading from the back of a cart, using a pitchfork – the muck is tossed up and then whacked with the fork
Turf	Peat cut into a rectangular shape and dried for fuel
Turmit	Turnip
Tussocky	Uneven ground caused by large clumps of grass
Urchin	Hedgehog
Vairn	Fern
Varmin	Vermin
Veelvare	Fieldfare
Vitnry	Veterinary surgeon
Vlat	Lad
Wim	Winnow
Wimmin dust	Chaff
Windhover	Kestrel
Withy vine	Bindweed, convolvulus
Wont	Mole
Wont heave	Mole hill
Wont snap	Mole trap
Worts, wortleberries	Bilberries
Yaffle	Green woodpecker
Zenvy	Wild mustard
Zool, zull	Plough (noun)
Zweal	Scorch or burn, as in burning bracken and heather to encourage new growth

After the revels at Barrington!
(Courtesy Somerset Archaeological and Natural History Society)

CHAPTER 7

The King and the Cakes

The following poem by Tommy Nutty provides examples of how the R and the vowel sound are transposed. Hence *great* becomes *gurt*, *run* becomes *urn*, *red* becomes *urd* and *Bridgwater* becomes *Burgewater*. This practice occurs several times in this description of King Alfred's most famous episode, the burning of the cakes, which took place near the Somerset village of Athelney. The original poem is much longer and only a selection of verses is given:

> Come hither, Zummerzetzhire voak, an lissen unto me,
> I tell o one whose neame to us a household word zhud be,
> 'Tis natal truth I'm gwine to tell, I've gleaned vrom deep-larned books,
> Vor I've picked up a thing or two zince vust I skared off rooks.
>
> Although I'm jist what zome voaks tarm a Zummerzetzhire vlat,
> I niver yet vound out much cause to be ashamed of that.
> To many a bright an gorgeous name on England's zcroll o vame,
> West country voak coud allus boast a purty decent claim;
>
> But brightest, bravest ov em all, old Zummerzet can zhow,
> The neame ov one who lived an died ten hundred years ago!
> Vrom Quantock round to Mendip long mid the praises ring,
> Ov noble book-larned Alfred, our Western warrior King!
>
> I zpose you know 'twar ztarmy times when he began to reign,
> An hordes o roving pirates comed vron out the narthern main.
> An ranzackted our country, both wi vire and wi zword,
> Oh yes, 'twar despurt times indeed – that 'twar upon my word.
>
> Then Alfred meade girt fighting zhips an zen em out to zea,
> That he upon the tossin waves a match vor em mid be.
> Twar ther he zhowed his measter mind – aah, he war var vrom daft,
> The cunning way he worked his zhips outmatched their Danish craft.

Then Alfred bound the varmints down – but lying words they zpoke,
A zet ov piecrust promises they purty zpeedy broke.
And then the King, droo trusting em, war uprepared d'ye zee?
Zo things turned all agen en like, as mid wi you or me.

His only zafety then it zims war in disguise an vlight,
Unknown an penniless, poor chap! he wandered day and night.
I've pictured en avore my eyes, as plain as if I zeed en,
Wi narry crown upon his head, but zich as nature gied en.

Well, he trudged on to Athelney, worn out an weak an thin,
Wur zome kind zoul, a varmer's wife, vor mussy took en in.
Lar bless her dear old kindly 'art, zhe bath'd his vevered head,
An zted of rushes, laid en on her own best veather bed,

But zims one day when he comed back vrom gallivanting roun,
They zet en watching ov zome ceakes a baking on the groun,
Left by hisself a little while his thoughts beginn'd to roam,
He thought of his dear loved ones left wi'out a house or home.

The missus in the dairy znuffed a kind of burning smell,
As quick as womin allus be – zhe guessed what 'twar right well.
Then creeping zoft on tippy-toe, zhee looked in droo the winder,
An zeed the King a znoring there, the ceakes burned to a zinder.

'Oh, drat thee, lazy bones,' she cried, 'an coosen 'tend to that,'
Then up went her gurt urd vat hand, an gied en zich a pat.
Poor chap, he tried to zay a word, but zhe cried, 'None o' thee zlack,
'Or else you mitching vagabond, I'll beat thee like a zack.

'Vor all the kindness thee'st received, a nice return to meake!
'Why, any babby twelve months old knows how to beake a ceake!
'I'm sure, if's bin the King hisself, we cooden do more vor thee,
'Yet coosen put thee vinger ztrait to do anything vor we.

'But zcritchy-zcratchy all day long thee'st zit wi pen an book,
'I'll burn the dratted thing, I will; don't gie I zich a look,
'An then the can'les thee dost waste a reading books in bed,
'I'll warn thee oosen care a straw if the roof burned auver 'ead.

'I've watched thee too when'st little thought, I've zeed thee zlat and
vling,
'An zwish the vlail-ztick like a zword, vor every martel thing,
'If oosent work, well goo an vight, 'twill zuit your addled brains,
'If like a long-dog dissen urn, as zoon as zeed the Danes.

'An now I think o' it, what's the cause you'm in zuch despurt hurry
'To zee the Holy Vather, when he comes vrom Glastonbury?
'No doubt thee'st got a heap ov zins thee'rt longin to confess,
'But I veel zure as how there is zome mystery in the mess.

'What, oosent budge?' then wi the same zhe vetched en zuch a
clinger,
Wi her vlat hand agen his ear – I 'zure 'ee 'twar a zlinger,
Then wi the zame zhe heard a zhout, an looking out it 'peers,
Zhe zeed a lot ov vighting men, wi girt long bows and zpears,

An zhoutin loud 'Long live the King!' in rushed these armèd men –
Poor zoul, zhe cooden do no more, but vainted there an then.
But zhe comed roun in coorse o' time, an to allay her vear,
The Holy Vather, he explained the matter all quite clear.

An then they had a jolly veast, an at the King's command,
The dame war honoured wi a zeat right close to his right hand.
Then Alfred in a noble zpeech returned his warmest thanks
Vor all her kindness, an he hoped zhe'd zcuse his voolish pranks.

From *The Somerset Folk Series Number 1, Selected Poems in Somerset Dialect*, pp 65–71; Somerset Folk Press, 1921.

QUIZ 1

See if you can decipher the following Somerset expressions. Clues are given in brackets. Answers at the bottom of the page.

1. Wha' be gwain 'ave? (Music to the ears)
2. Whirr zer bin to? (A directional request)
3. S'right nottlin, sno. Spec me rumatics'll zoon be yer. (Expecting colder weather)
4. S'getting dimpsey so you d'mind y'doan go vallin auver they ruckles on yer way cross mower (Caution is needed on the peat moors at dusk).
5. Eye sorer war shin. (Observation of Monday morning activity)
6. Cordin eye, stimey wenoam. (Heard at chucking out time)
7. Ow beyon, meeyole muckers? (A friendly health check)
8. Ouzes this is scrum pee? (Confusion over ownership of drinks)
9. Dough-knee get 'ammered. (Fatherly advice)
10. My azwell gwoam. (No point in staying)

Quiz 1 Answers

1. What are you going to have?
2. Where has he been?
3. It's really cold, you know. I expect my rheumatism will soon be here.
4. It's just getting dark so mind you don't fall over the peat stacks on your way across the moor.
5. I saw her washing.
6. According to me, it's time he went home.
7. How are you, my friends of long standing.
8. To whom does this cider belong? (Whose is this scrumpy?)
9. Don't get drunk!
10. Might as well go home.

CHAPTER 8

Zyder Tawk

Cider is so deeply rooted in Somerset culture that it has inevitably developed a language of its own with many words of the local dialect being unique to cider making. The varieties of apples reflect the Somerset links, with names like Kingston Black (from Kingston St Mary near Taunton), Stembridge Jersey and Yarlington Mill. Other varieties continue the theme: Ashton Bitter, Backwell Red, Bath Russet, Beauty of Bath, Beauty of Wells, Bridgwater Pippin, Burrow Hill Early, Camelot, Cheddar Permain, Chisel Jersey, Coat Jersey (Coat is near Martock), Coker Seedling, Fair Maid of Taunton, Lambroook Pippin, Nailsea White, Pennard Bitter, Taunton Golden Pippin and Yeovil Sour.

An orchard is traditionally planted with standard trees to allow cattle and sheep to graze beneath them for nine months of the year. These trees are usually grown from cuttings grafted onto a strong root stock such as a Crab Apple. Occasionally, especially when developing new varieties, gribbles are planted in the 'orchet'. Prior to the time that the fruit ripens, the cattle and sheep are removed from the orchard. There is an expression on the Mendip Hills that states that you *must allas hain-up come Priddy Vair*, which comes towards the end of August.

Gribbles	Seedlings
Hain	Leave a meadow to grow
Orchet	Orchard

At harvest time, the apples are gathered in. At one time this was carried out by the women and children (they could bend over repeatedly better than the men), who collected the fruit from the orchard floor in their aprons or in a picker basket holding a peck. These were then tipped into woolly butts (or maunds on Exmoor where there is a lack of willow to provide the withy canes) and taken to the cider mill for pressing. Fruit still on the trees would be poled to bring them to the ground. Griggling would bring in a smaller, second batch. Collecting this second batch was often more hazardous. Fallen fruit, which has bruised and softened, and fruit that has come, is particularly attractive to apple drames and young lads who go scrumping or snobbing.

Apple drame	Wasp
Come	Ripe – apples are left to 'come' before being gathered
Griggling	Harvesting the remainder of the apples from the trees in an orchard after the main crop has been brought in
Maund	Oval baskets made of ash staves
Peck	About 20 lb in weight
Poled	Shaken down from the trees with poles
Scrumping, Snobbing	Pinching apples from an orchard
Woolly butt	2 handled basket made of withy

The gathered apples are then taken to a storage area, typically a loft in a barn. From there, they are milled; crushed to form a pomace. The evidence of horse gin mills can occasionally be found in old barns where the circle worked by the horses can still be seen. In some mills, the pomace is collected in a bow.

Bow	Square wooden container, constructed from elm, for collecting pomace or pummy under the mill
Horse gin	A mill where a horse turns a wheel, which is connected by a series of cogs to drive rollers which crush the apples
Pomace or pummy	Crushed apple ready for pressing, or the left over apple and straw after pressing
Scatter mill	A mill which uses two cast iron rollers with interlocking pegs and sockets

Before the crushed apples are pressed to create the apple juice, the container which collects the juice needs to be primmed up. The crushed apples and layers of reeds are laid down to form lissoms and set the cheese. One layer on another is laid down until around a ton in weight has been used to create a cheese.

Cheese	The mass of apple and straw laid in layers ready for pressing
Lissom	A layer of reeds and pomace
Prim up	Block up any gaps in the collecting dish to prevent leakage – this used to be done with clay if available or wool and dung if not – water is added to swell the wooden

	tray until the gaps seal and the temporary fillers are then removed
Reeds	Combed, cleaned wheat straw

A vollyer or hatch is then placed on top of the cheese to provide an even pressure when the pressing starts. The collected juices will than be transferred to casks on a horsing, perhaps using a tundish or tunnacre. Hogsheads are most common but butts or pipes are sometimes used.

Butt or pipe	120 gallon cask, pipes are tall and butts short
Hogshead	54 gallon cask
Horsing	Stand used to keep casks off the ground
Tundish or tunnacre	Wooden funnel used to transfer the juice into the casks
Vollyer or hatch	Heavy square block of wood

Now begins the serious process of fermentation during which so much can go wrong – with muthery or summery cider being produced instead of good quality scrumpy. The brewer also needs to keep a careful watch to avoid the cider tissing or going tuzzilly.

Cheese ready for pressing

Muther	Unwanted jelly-like substance that sometimes appears in cider
Muthery	Containing muther
Scrumpy	Good quality cider
Summery	Acidic, when the cider is too sharp
Tissing, tuzzilly	Fermenting too rapidly

And now, all that is left to do is to fill your firkin and enjoy the fruits of your labour. Remember that, in moderation, cider is a healthy drink and can keep the body in good working order. Wassail!

Old Zam could niver goafer long
Wi'out ees jar ur virkin;
'Er used the zider zame as oyul
T'keep ees joints vrum quirkin'.

Firkin	Half gallon cider jar
Wassail	Good health to you (Anglo-Saxon and used as a drinking toast)

However, excess can lead to various states of drunkenness:

Half skimmished	Approaching drunkenness, one or two more pints will do it
Skimmished	Drunk, merry but coherent and able to walk home
Cidered up	Drunk, incoherent but still able to walk home
'Ammered	Drunk, incoherent and incapable of walking home but knows it
Smashed	Drunk, incoherent, unable to walk home and too drunk to know it
Wrecked	Drunk, unconscious, incapable of knowing anything and unlikely to know it for at least a week

and of course there's another name for cider, which should not be forgotten:

Tone Vale Tea	Tone Vale Hospital in past years was notorious as a mental institution.

Pork in Cider

Having familiarised yourself with the language of cider, perhaps you'd like now to familiarise yourself with cider as a culinary ingredient. The recipe requires just half a pint of cider and begs the question 'What do I do with the other half?' Well, you could save it to go with the meal! Cider is used throughout Somerset as a marinade, especially for the cheaper cuts of meat. An overnight soaking helps to break down the meat fibres during the cooking process. Try the following:

4 pork chops
1 large onion chopped
2 eating apples, peeled, cored and diced
½ pint cider
¼ pint stock
3 oz butter
2 oz flour

Coat the pork chops in flour (seasoned with salt and pepper if desired) and fry in the butter until brown. Place the chops to one side and use the same pan to fry the diced apple and onion until both are softened. Stir in the remainder of the flour, cook for just one minute and then slowly add the cider and stock. Bring to the boil, return the chops into the pan and simmer for half an hour until cooked. Serve with new potatoes and fresh vegetables.

CHAPTER 9

Ghostes

Varmer Pearce said to I, 'Do you believe in ghostes?' and I said, 'Not wi'out I do zee 'em vor my own zelf, an' I never zeed one but once. Have you zeed one, Varmer Pearce?' And he zaid, 'No, but they have a-got the tale that there's one do bide in thik empty house up top o' parish.' He zaid they did hear un knockin' at night times; and Miller Biggin's brother's wife's father heard un when he wer' gwain home-along one night late.

But it d'zim that's a long way round for hearzay. Gwain home late! Zo I should think! But 'tis always a job to meet wi' anybiddy that have a-zeed a ghost; 'tis always somebiddy some kin to 'em that have a-zeed un. An' I be always dubious about volk that do zee or hear things late at night; they be always in too much o' a hirry to ask questions.

Years agone Zolomon Tipple wer' supposed to have zeed a ghost comin' down Gallinton Hill, wi' chains a clankin', an eyes so big as tea-sassers. Zolomon runned vor the life o' un; and what wer' it after all? Miller Biggin's wold white hoss wi' a chain on the lag o' un to kip un vrom runnin' away when they did want to catch un. That were the ghost wi' chains a-clankin'; and as for eyes like tea-sassers – if Zolomon had zaid quart-cups, that odd a-bin more in his line; and if he had'n a-bid so long at The Wheatsheaf, I sim he ooden a-zeed no ghostes at all!

Now Jakey Green wer' always a terrible feller vor zeein' things. Why, one night he wanted to make I believe he could zee two moons shinin' in my pond; and then when he got home, he coulden zee his own garden hatch. One day, I do mind, I sent un to market wi' a drove o' pigs. An' the zame day, after he wer' a-gone, some men come and fixed up a finger-post at the cross-roads, an' painted un white all over. Jakey had to bring home zix calves, and he must ha' bid about, vor it wer' dark night when ee got back; and he runned into house wi' a face so white as a sheet. No, I wunt tell a lie; vor no-biddy ever zeed Jakey wi' a white face! But he ood a-bin white if he had a-chanced to a-bin clean.

'What's the matter wi'ee, Jakey?' I said, 'Anybiddy ood think you had a-met wi' the Wold Nick, or zeed a ghost.' 'Zo I have, Maester; he do stand at the cross-roads wi' his arms a-strout.' Then I guessed what wer' the matter!

'Where's the calves?' I zaid.

'I left 'em, zir, an' runned vor my life athirt the fields. Do 'ee gie me the leastest drop o' brandy, zir.'

'Brandy!' I zaid. 'Put thy zilly fools head under the pump, I got a mind!'

Then I had un out to the cross-roads, an' made un goo right up to the post, an' touch un wi' his vinger, an' Jakey did shake an' tremble all the time.

'There, Jakey, next time when thee dost zee anything thee hast never zeed avore, thee take my advice, an' open thy eyes avore thee dost open thy mouth.'

It took Jakey half the night to find the calves, an' I sim he wished he had'n bin in sich a hirry to zee a ghost that warden there. But I'll tell 'ee about the ghost I zeed my own self. Years agone, little Benny Snooks hanged himself wi' a zarin' rope to one of the apple-trees in Little Orchet. They did use to say that his ghost did walk there; an' one day Jakey put it about that he had a-zeed un, an' did groan-y enough to make your blood rin cold.

Well, one night when I wer goin' upstairs I chanced to look out o' window, an' I thought I could zee summat in orchet quiet like, an' just as I got near the Tom Pud-tree I could zee summat hanging vrom the bough – an' all at once it zet up zich a groanin' as you never heard the likes o'. I listened for a bit, an' it come into my head that Benny Snooks used to have a terrible squeaky voice, but this wer' a gruffish noise. Zoo I went up to the tree, an' if you can believe what I do zay there wer' thik varmint o' Jakey up in the tree, a-helpin' hiszelf to the best o' the apples, an' putting 'em in the zack he had a-hung up. I tell 'ee, Jakey an' I had a vew words thik night. Tidden worth while vor I to tell 'ee what I zaid to un, an' Jakey idden likely to tell 'ee vor hiszelf. But Benny Snooks' ghost han't a-walked since. An' that's the only ghost as ever I zeed!

An extract from *Down-Along Talks* by Dan'l Grainger (David J Gass); Somerset Folk Press, 1922.

Porlock Weir

CHAPTER 10

Adge Cutler and the Wurzels

Without doubt, Adge Cutler and the Wurzels have done more to introduce Somerset dialect to the world at large than anyone one else in the county. Those who previously were unaware of the sound of the Somerset tongue were suddenly singing along with such lines as 'Zhe ups an' zlips and zummat rips' and 'Ooh ar! Ooh ar!'

When I found myself working in the Midlands and the north of England, my colleagues would recognise my Somerset accent and then proffer such queries as 'Did you bring any cider with you?' or, more sarcastically, 'Is that your combine harvester parked outside?' The latter seems such an odd question but both are direct references to songs that made the national charts in the late 1960s, *Drink up thee Cider, Twice Daily* and *I Got a Brand New Combine 'Arvester*, recorded by Adge Cutler and the Wurzels.

It all began in 1966 at the Royal Oak pub in Nailsea. In Liverpool, a similar sensation was going on with with a 4-piece band wearing smart suits and 'Beatle' haircuts. Those Liverpudlians took the world by storm but finished as a band many years ago. In the parallel universe of Somerset, Alan John (Adge) Cutler took to the stage at the Royal Oak with the Wurzels. Their dung-covered boots, haystack hairstyles and ever present cider jars formed a stark contrast to the northern smoothies.

Adge grabbed the microphone and performed *Twice Daily*. All those present knew that here was something very different and very special. 'Scrumpy and Western' music was born that night and Somerset was taken by storm. And looking back, whilst the Wurzels lacked the international spotlight acquired by the Merseyside beat group, in Somerset, the Avonside 'beet' group can at least claim to still be going strong.

It was in June 1966 that Adge Cutler met agent John Miles. In November of that year EMI record producer Bob Barratt was at the Royal Oak as Adge Cutler and the Wurzels took to the straw-strewn stage clutching their pints of cider. They were introduced to rapturous applause from the audience. As the noise subsided, Adge looked at the producer and asked, 'Is it rolling, Bob?' Shortly after, EMI released a double 'A' sided single with *Twice Daily* and *Drink up thee Cider*.

The Wurzels take their medicine twice daily

Drink up thee cider, Drink up thee cider,
For tonight we'll merry be, merry be,
We'll knock the milk churns over,
An' roll 'em in the clover,
The corn's alf-cut and so be we.

Wonderful lyrics! Locally the song shot to the top of the charts and nationally reached number 45 in a rare occurrence of a regional record breaking into the national arena. Success was then guaranteed when the BBC banned its performance on TV due to the sensitivity of such lyrics in *Twice Daily* as 'Zhe ups an' zlips and zummat rips, and I went there twice daily'. Following the ban, the BBC was inundated with requests to play the less sensitive *Drink up thee Cider*, which soon became recognised as the national anthem for Somerset. It has been sung with great gusto at birthday parties, dances, weddings, and even funerals, ever since. Such was the demand that the BBC programmes such as *Two Way Family Favourites*, *Workers' Playtime*, *Housewives' Choice* and many others were under

pressure to play the record. The Wurzels took to the road and performed all over the country.

During the PACAW years (pre-Adge Cutler and the Wurzels), Somerset drinking folk had little choice but to sing other people's songs: *Danny Boy*, *Maybe It's Because I'm a Londoner*, *It's a Long Way to Tipperary* and the like. But they now had songs of their own, in their own dialect, which made them much easier to sing at the end of a heavy night's drinking. No longer did the evenings finish with a rendition of *Show Me the Way to Go Home*. Instead, they finished with dignity as all present rose to sing Somerset's new national anthem, *Drink up thee Cider*. Those were the days.

Sadly Adge, known as the Bard of Avonmouth, died in May 1974 in a car accident near Chepstow, and Somerset was deprived of one of its great characters. But his music lives on and, I am pleased to say, the Wurzels continue to entertain West Country audiences and still produce songs in the Somerset dialect, perhaps the best known being *Combine Harvester*, a parody of Melanie's *Brand New Key*. Coupled with the 'B' side *Blackbird*, it soon reached number 1 in both the UK and Canada. Throughout the 70s and 80s their success continued with more records, such as *Cider Drinker*, *Farmer Bill's Cowman* and *Give Me England*. National tours, performances in Tenerife, Cyprus and the Middle East, two tours of Canada and an increasing number of television appearance on programmes such as *The Basil Brush Show*, *Crackerjack*, *That's Life* and *Seaside Special* all contributed to a busy, showbiz lifestyle, quite unfamiliar to these Somerset lads.

Reflecting back on the Beatles, we can see how, over the years, they lost much of their Liverpool dialect. Billy Connolly, that great Glaswegian comedian, likewise tempered his strong dialect in order to be understood on an international level. In contrast, the Wurzels never lost theirs and have spread the word far and wide. These wonderful exponents of 'Scrumpy and Western' have done much to educate the rest of the world in the dialect of Somerset and to keep the language alive.

Wassail to the Wurzels!

CHAPTER 11

Somerset Place Names

Somerset is full of wonderful place names. Allow your thoughts to run riot with Nempnett Thrubwell, Gurney Slade, Compton Pauncefoot, Cricket Malherbie, Keinton Mandeville. Aren't they splendid? Many of these double-name places carry a Norman influence, from after the days of the Norman Conquest. Stogursey was once Stoke de Courcey, reflecting the Saxon origins of Stoke and then the French ownership of the de Courcey family. Farleigh Hungerford was once in the ownership of the Hungerford family. Brympton d'Evercy, Cheddon Fitzpaine, Orchard Wyndham, Wootton Courtney and Norton Fitzwarren provide further examples.

Following this theme of the use of Saxon words linked with Norman names, the best but least obvious example is Bridgwater. It is nothing to do with bridges or water. In AD 800 there was no river bridge where Bridgwater now stands. There was a quayside. The Saxon word for quayside is *bryjg*. Hence there is no 'e' on the end of Bridg. The town, after 1066, came under the ownership of Walter de Douai, a French lord. So it became Walter's quayside, Bridg of Walter, corrupted to Bridgwater. So now if anyone asks you why there is no 'e' in the middle of Bridgwater, you can explain that it is the 'l' from Walter that is actually missing.

This mix of Anglo-Saxon and Norman can be found across Somerset but it is perhaps in the shorter place names that we can find those whose Saxon influence affects the local dialect. Aller (from alder) and Ash reflect the Saxon names of trees. Beer, which is not far from Othery, is Anglo-Saxon for a woodland that produces acorns and beechmast for feeding cattle and pigs. Coincidentally, and as if trying to disprove my Anglo-Saxon theory, the hamlet next to Beer is called Stout!

Other Anglo-Saxon names survive:

Cleeve	Steep slope
Ham	Enclosure
Hay	Hedge
Hewish, Huish	From *hiwisc*, a homestead
Lang	Long, as in Langport
Meare	Pond

Oare	Slope
Perry	Pear tree
Sleight, slate	Sheep pasture, common on the Mendips
Steart	Peninsula of land
Wick	Commonly held farm
Worth	Private farm, as in Huntworth

When *worth* is found in a place name, it is normally preceded by a person's name to indicate to whom the farm belonged, eg Huntworth – Hunt's farm – Gupworthy, Clatworthy and so on. In similar fashion, Huntspill is derived from Hunt's Pill, a pill being a little creek or safe harbour for small boats. The word can also be found in Crowpill, an area on the edge of Bridgwater, and Pill in the north of the county.

In names such as Chedzoy, Middlezoy and Westonzoyland, the Saxon word *zoy* indicates the presence of an island. Each of these settlements, known collectively as the Zoy villages, lies in the low lying area of Sedgemoor and each is on ground that stands sufficiently proud of the surrounding area to have once been an island during times of flood, which was frequent before serious drainage was introduced to the moors. In the case of Chedzoy, the area once belonged to a Saxon named Cheppa, and hence it was Cheppa's Zoy.

The pronunciation of Somerset place names also requires some clarification, and perhaps this should be passed on to television newsreaders who frequently appear to lack the local knowledge.

Aisholt	*Ashult*
Brean	*Breeyun*
Carhampton	*Cram'ton*
Chedzoy	The pronounciation is *Chedzee* to those who live in the village, *Chidgey* to folk from Bridgwater
Combwich	*Cummidge*
Coxley	*Coaks-lee*
Crewkerne	*Crook-urn*
Hatch Beauchamp	*Hatch Beecham*
Leigh on Mendip	*Lye*
Middlezoy	*Middlezee*
Othery	*Oatheree* (not as in otter)
Pawlett	*Pollutt* (Poll as in Polly)
Stawell	*Stall*
Tintinhull	*Tint'null*
Weston-super-Mare	*Wessun*

CHAPTER 12

Country Calendar

Even today there are many traditional Somerset rural practices that are as old as the dialect itself. Most involve the active participation of long established Somerset families and hence they provide particularly good opportunites to hear the surviving dialect. Fortunately they cover the whole year and thus provide regular opportunities to discover the local tongue.

January

Plough Sunday

On the first Sunday after 6th January, Plough Sunday is celebrated on a rotation basis at one of five churches centred on Nunney. At the early evening service, a traditional plough is blessed. The congregation later shares bread, cheese and cider.

Wassail

Cider has long been part of the social fabric of Somerset life. One of the county's oldest surviving traditions is that of wassailing on the Old Twelfth Night, 17th January, each year. Twelfth Night is generally considered to be 6th January but in medieval times the calendar was adjusted, resulting in the change of date. Traditions such as wassailing were so deep in the culture of Somerset folk that it was felt important to continue the practice on the same night each year despite the calendar shift, hence 17th January. Wassailing is perhaps Somerset's oldest tradition, dating back at least to the pre-Roman pagan times.

The word wassail comes from the Anglo-Saxon *waes hael* – good health to you. The tradition still survives, most notably at the Butchers Arms at Carhampton (Cram'ton, of course). The wassailing ceremony is carried out in the orchard where the youngest person places cake or toast soaked in cider in the forks of a tree, traditionally the oldest tree, and then a bucket of cider spiced with nutmeg and ginger is poured onto the roots and the wassailing song begins:

Oh apple tree we wassail thee
And happily wilt thou bear,
For the Lord doth know where we shall be
Till apples another year.

To bloom well and to bear well
So merry let us be,
Let every man take off his hat
And shout out to th'old apple tree.

The following chorus is then shouted:

Oh apple tree! We wassail thee!
And hoping thou will bear
Hatsful, capsful, three bushel bagsful
And a little heap under the stair.

This is immediately followed by the traditional three cheers and gunshot is fired through the branches of the apple trees to frighten away the evil spirits and ensure a prosperous crop in the ensuing year. All present then retire to the bar for a night's serious celebration, which will definitely include cider and may include a Wassail punch.

Wassail Punch

1 gallon cider
2 pints of orange juice
1 cup lemon juice
24 whole cloves
4 sticks of cinnamon
1 cup of sugar

Put the cider, orange juice, lemon and sugar in a large cooking pot. Place the cloves and cinnamon in a clean cloth bag and suspend in the pot of liquid. Simmer for around 12 to 15 minutes, but do not allow to boil. Remove the spice bag and serve in warm mugs.

Winter Weather

Winters on Mendip and Exmoor can be extremely hard. Those of 1940, 1947 and 1963 saw entire communities snowed in for weeks on end. The following is a reference to a bumblebee (drumble-drone) and a wasp (apple-drame) who failed to survive a hard moorland winter:

> *An apple-drame and a drumble-drone*
> *Were all there wert to see.*
> *The apple-drame lay dead in the snow*
> *The drumble-drone in the tree.*

From Exmoor comes another hint of hard weather, together with a reference to snails (snarley horns) and hardship (barley bread is of poor quality):

> *Snarley orn put out your orn,*
> *Vather and mother's daid,*
> *Zester an' brother be at the back door,*
> *A-begging for barley bread.*

Vivary Park, Taunton

February

St Valentine's Day

Pagan practices pre-date St Valentine's Day. It was once believed that 14th February was the day that the birds chose their mates and across the county there were various techniques for selecting partners for that day. Typically a dance would be

held and some method or other of drawing lots would be devised to pair couples. When Christianity was introduced, the Church tried to abolish the pagan practice but it was far too popular! All they could do was to legitimise it by linking it to a Christian saint. St Valentine was the saint whose saint's day fell the closest.

In Somerset, one tradition associated with this period was the use of an apple to identify a future partner. The apple was be peeled by a young woman, in such a way as to keep the skin in one long strand. This would then be thrown backwards over her shoulder and allowed to land. The shape formed by the peel would be translated into a letter, which would be the initial of the man she would marry.

Collop Monday

The day before Shrove Tuesday. Collop is a Somerset word for salted meat, and this was to be used up before Lent. Collop Monday is also associated with *crocking* or *drownin' o' cloam*, the custom of throwing broken crockery into the street or into someone's house, often as much as a complete sackful. The general idea was for the young lads to hurl a load of broken crockery into someone's front room or kitchen and disappear undetected into the darkness as they shouted: 'Tippetty tappety toe, give me a pancake and then I'll go.'

In some villages, perhaps where there was a lack of crockery, dirt or stones would do. These would be thrown at the front door with the words: 'Tippetty tappetty tin, give me a pancake and I will come in.' If the perpetrators were caught, they would either be invited in to eat pancake or they would have their faces blackened as a punishment. Rather like 'trick or treat', it has never been popular with the adults and it is easy to understand how it has disappeared.

The dialect word lenshard has its origins in this practice, being formed from 'Lent shard', the shard being a reference to the pieces of broken crockery.

Shrove Tuesday – Egg Shackling

Egg shackling is a tradition that survives in very few Somerset villages. Shepton Beauchamp and Stoke St Gregory schools provide good examples. Egg shackling is a game for children and is played in one of two ways. In the first method, eggs are hard boiled and then decorated. Two children at a time then crack their eggs against each other. Usually one cracks and the other survives. This continues until only one egg is left. The Somerset practice is more commonly to take raw eggs, one from each of the children, put them in a sieve and roll them. One by one they crack and the winner is the child whose egg survives unscathed the longest. Even that one has then to be cracked to prove that it wasn't hard-boiled.

Another old custom associated with Shrove Tuesday is 'throwing at cocks', which fortunately has died out. This was the practice of pitching sticks and stones at a cockerel until it was dead. There was a cockpit at Wiveliscombe and there is a Coxpit Farm at East Bower near Bridgwater, both of which appear to have had their origins in cock fighting.

March

Mothering Sunday and Easter Processions

In Milverton, mothers join hands on Mothering Sunday and walk around the church. Simnel cake is then shared. At Glastonbury, there are religious pilgrimages at Eastertime with processions through the streets.

Sedgemoor Rabbit

As Easter approaches, our thoughts turn to the spring and its associations, such as Easter eggs and the Easter bunnies. Rabbits are of course present throughout the year, nowhere more so than around the fields of Sedgemoor, and they formed an important part of the diet in Somerset's village communities. Not only did their capture help to keep down what country folk can only see as vermin, but it put meat on the table. You may enjoy the following recipe for Sedgemoor rabbit:

> *2 rabbits, cut into serving pieces*
> *Flour seasoned with salt and pepper*
> *2 tablespoons of cooking oil*
> *2 onions, chopped*
> *6 rashers of unsmoked bacon, chopped*
> *6 carrots, peeled and coined*
> *¼ pound of mushrooms, sliced*
> *½ pint of chicken stock*
> *½ pint of cider*
> *2 tablespoons of fresh parsley*
> *Pinch of oregano, pinch of thyme*
> *4 bay leaves*

Preheat oven to 350° F, 177° C, gas mark 4. Toss the rabbit pieces in a tablespoon of seasoned flour and brown in a pan of hot vegetable oil. Transfer to a casserole. Part boil the carrots while you cook the onions and bacon together in the pan until the onions are soft and stir in another tablespoon of seasoned flour. Add the chicken stock and cider and bring to the boil. Add this mix to the casserole along with the carrots and sliced mushrooms. Add herbs according to taste. Cook

in the oven for 1½ hours, or longer if required, until the rabbit is tender. Remove the bay leaves before serving. Ideal accompaniments are new potatoes and fresh vegetables.

April

April is the month when nesting birds are at their most active. Naturally birds and beasts feature strongly in folklore, not least being the robin.

Who so robs the Ruddick's nest
Neither prospers nor is blest.

Candle auctions

April begins with the Daffodil Rally at Mells. Then, on the first Tuesday after 6th April, a 'secret' candle auction is held at the thatched Olde Poppe Inn in Tatworth. There are 25 rights to bid for the grazing on Stowel Mead. These rights are held by the members of the Stowel Court, some of whom hold more than one right. Refreshments, after the bidding is complete, include watercress from the meadow. The auction requires an inch-long half-inch tallow candle, which is placed on a wooden board. This is then suspended from the ceiling in such a way that the bidders are unable to see the state of the candle. The last bid before the candle expires is the winning bid.

A similar candle auction is held at the Manor Inn at Chedzoy. Land called Church Acre is auctioned there once every 21 years.

The month closes with the Hobby Hoss ceremony in Minehead on the last day of the month, a practice which continues ...

May

Minehead Hobby Hoss

The ceremony starts in Minehead at 6 am on the first day of May. It then makes its way to Whitecross and continues on to Dunster for the afternoon. The Hoss looks nothing like a horse, although it has a tail. The creature is about eight feet long and boat shaped and is worn around a local volunteer, suspended by shoulder straps. The wearer is hidden by a mask made out of tin and is crowned with ribbons and feathers. The top half of the Hoss is bedecked in ribbons and circles. At the rear end comes the tail, which is swished around to beat anyone foolish enough to venture too close.

Minehead Hobby Hoss at Dunster Castle

The Hoss, whose original purpose appears to have been to frighten off Viking invaders, is accompanied by musicians and 'Gullivers', gentlemen who wear masks, tall hats and ribbons. Their job is to collect money for charitable causes, which they do with great enthusiasm. Needless to say, they visit numerous pubs in the course of their journey. At one time they used large cudgels and would enter people's homes and demand money. They were quite prepared to club anyone not responding as requested – fortunately such a practice has long since ceased.

June

The end of May and the beginning of June bring the famous Bath and West Show. Although this is modern in style, its origins go back to much smaller shows in the towns and villages of the county. Whilst the show has something for everyone, a visit to the sheep and cattle exhibits offers the opportunity to meet country folk with wonderful Somerset dialects.

It is also an excellent venue for experiencing Somerset culinary specialities, with numerous marquees providing opportunities for tasting. Somerset has a close association with certain types of food. Cider and apples, Cheddar cheese and strawberries, pork and the less well known whortleberries. Historically elvers

Girls working in the peat diggings

once formed an annual delight, dipped in flour and fried like whitebait, but now elver stocks are rapidly declining through over-fishing. Prices have soared and this local delicacy rarely reaches the plates of Somerset folk.

July

Priddy Fair, not to be confused with the sheep fair that comes later in the year, and further pilgrimages at Glastonbury are just two of the public events in July. This is also a good month for picking wortleberries, which grow wild on the hills and moors.

Whortleberry Pie

Whortleberries grow all over the Quantock Hills and Exmoor and make an excellent pie. Indeed such an excellent pie that for decades there was a tradition of serving whortleberry pie to the Australian cricket team whenever they visited Somerset. The tradition went back to 1938, even before the days of Don Bradman. During their stay, when the Aussies put up at the Castle Hotel in Taunton, they would enjoy their whortleberry feast. However, in 1991 Steve Waugh's team decided not to stay at the Castle Hotel as it lacked both a swimming pool and gymnasium – and thus ended the whortleberry pie tradition for the Australian team. Sadly they seem to be managing even better without it!

These small blue-berried plants lie close to ground and can be found mainly in the wooded coombes rather than the open moorland. They are small, so a large number need to be collected, and are quite sharp, hence the need to sweeten with a cup of sugar. Late July and August are the best months for picking them.

2 rounds of pastry, 9" in diameter
4 cups of whortleberries
1 tablespoon lemon juice
½ teaspoon grated lemon rind
1 cup sugar
Pinch of salt
¼ cup plain flour
Knob of butter

Preheat the oven to 425° F, 215° C, gas mark 7. Line a 9" pie dish with pastry. Wash and drain the berries and place them in a large bowl with the other ingredients, except the pastry. Mix the ingredients together and pour into the

lined pie dish. Spread the butter across the contents in small lumps. Roll out the top crust and place over the filling to fit as a lid. Crimp the lower and upper pastry circles to join them together. Use a knife to insert 4 slots in the upper crust to allow the steam to escape. Place the pie on a sheet of tin foil in case the juices boil over. Bake for about 35 minutes until the crust is golden. Serves around 6 people.

August

Haymaking

One of the busiest of times for farming folk, haymaking also gives an excuse for sociability. Before mechanisation, gathering in the hay was a hugely time-consuming task and even the children would have to pull their weight. For this reason, school record books across the county show how, in the years before the war, it was normal for the majority of schoolchildren to be absent during the haymaking period.

With so many of the community involved, it became a grand social gathering, when gallons of cider would be consumed. Stone firkin jars, wrapped in a protective layer of wicker, would be left to soak in streams to keep them cool, or placed down rabbit holes when no streams were available. The workforce would head out to the fields with their wide-brimmed hats to keep the sun off, their lunch pack of bread, cheese and apple, and their jar or barrel of cider. It was a long, hard day, and they often worked from dawn to dusk. All those involved deserved the harvest suppers, which were soon to follow.

Harvest Homes

There is so much going on in August that the visitor is spoilt for choice. Throughout August and September, villages hold their Harvest Home suppers, an annual gathering to celebrate the end of the harvest. One of the largest of these in Somerset is the East Brent Harvest Home. Large marquees enclose long rows of tables on which the harvest supper is served. Huge hams, plentiful local cheeses and a great deal of cider and beer are consumed.

Sheepdog Trials

Also throughout August, sheepdog trials are held in Somerset, especially at the western end of the county on the hills of Exmoor.

Lowland Games

In early August the Lowland Games are held at Thorney, near Langport, where the traditional games include events such as Welly Throwing and Mud Wrestling. These games lack the formality of their Highland counterparts, but are considerably more enjoyable as a consequence.

Steart Island Swim

At Burnham-on-Sea there is the annual swim from the beach across the muddy mouth of the River Parrett to Steart Island. This is not for the faint hearted. The Parrett is tidal and a strong current flows across its mouth – and the swim should only be attempted by the strongest of swimmers.

Steart Island is a low lying island in the mouth of the river, normally reserved just for the birds which use it as a safe haven, especially for waders and wildfowl including the huge flocks of shelduck that winter there.

Priddy Sheep Fair

Priddy Sheep Fair takes place on the Wednesday before 21st August each year. Priddy is a medieval village with a 13th century church overlooking the triangular village green on which the fair is held. In 1348 the plague hit the nearby city of Wells and the sale of sheep was transferred to Priddy, where it has survived ever since. Apart from sheep, ponies are also sold here, mostly by the travelling community. A separate area is now fenced off in which the ponies are traded. This is to keep the general public away from the animals in the interest of safety. A small funfair enhances the occasion.

The Priddy Oggy – the Somerset Pasty

Absolutely nothing to do with August, but Priddy Sheep Fair provides a convenient link to Priddy Oggies. Priddy was once at the heart of the lead mining industry on the Mendips. Pasties were perhaps one of the first convenience foods, especially for those miners. There are two versions, the Cornish Tiddy Oggy and the North Somerset Priddy Oggy. The former is shaped like a capital letter D lying on its side with the crimped pastry crust around the curved part of the D. The Priddy Oggy has the crimped crust across the top like the ridge of a roof.

In whichever form it was produced, the miners would eat their meal by holding the crimped crust. The Cornish miners clutched their curved D with both hands, like playing a harmonica. The Mendip miners held the knuckles of the pasty at each end. Once the meal had been eaten, and only the pastry that had been handled was left, the 'handles' would be discarded. The lead mines of Mendip and the tin mines of Cornwall held toxic chemicals such as cadmium and arsenic.

Throwing away the crust reduced the risk of toxic poisoning.

The recipe below is the way my mother made her pasties, and she always insisted on one thing: only cook with the best beef and never use minced or ground beef, which sadly we see in so many shop-bought pasties.

The pastry

> 1 lb plain flour
> ½ lb butter
> Pinch of salt, water

Rub the fat into the flour to form a coarse mixture. Add the salt and slowly add the water to mix into a ball. Put in a cool place.

The filling

> 1 lb beef, not stewing beef
> Potato
> Swede
> Small onion
> Salt and pepper, Knob of butter

Cut the steak into small chunks. Dice the potato and swede to form chunks about ½ inch across. Chop the onion finely. Roll out the pastry to about ¼ inch thick. Using a plate, cut out circles from the pastry and moisten the edges with water. Put a quarter of the steak and a quarter of the vegetables into the centre of the pastry circle, keeping it away from the edges and avoiding overfilling it. Add salt and pepper to taste, a small knob of butter and sprinkle the whole with flour. Fold the pastry from opposite sides of the circle by lifting two sides so that they join over the filling to create a ridge along the length of the pasty. Crimp the join and pierce the upper surface of the pastry to give a 1 inch cut to allow the steam to escape while cooking. Brush the pasty with beaten egg and bake in a hot oven (435° F, 220° C, gas mark 7) for about 20 minutes then reduce temperature to 325° F, 160° C, gas mark 3 for a further 40 minutes.

There are some schools of thought that a Priddy Oggy should correctly have a pork and cheese filling. You may like to try this by using the following alternative filling:

> 1 lb pork tenderloin, sliced into strips   3 oz grated Cheddar
> 2 rashers of bacon, chopped   1 teaspoon of sage

This filling could be bound together using a beaten egg.

September

September Fairs

The second Monday in September brings us Glastonbury's Tor Fair, a week long funfair which commenced life in the 12th century and for most of that time was a significant gathering for the sale of sheep, horses and cattle. Held on the side of Glastonbury Tor, its high visibility acted as an advertisment for its presence.

Frome's Cheese Fair comes on the last Wednesday in the month. Coincidentally, the last Wednesday also heralds the first day of Bridgwater Fair, the largest funfair in the area, which also dates back several hundred years. For the traditionalist, the Wednesday morning is the best time to visit Bridgwater Fair, to see the sheep and pony sales. The remaining three days are totally dedicated to the massive heart stopping rides.

Of course, having been to the fair, one would hope to get home safe and sound. Many travellers had to cross over rivers, which were quite often swollen by September rains. The following lines refer to the belief that rivers have a spirit of their own and are greedy when it comes to human life. Notice the double past tense *drownded*, so common in Somerset dialect and not just there for poetic correctness.

> *'Wur be maister?' zays the river.*
> *'Wur be Pony? zays the well.*
> *'I've atook 'n,' zays the water,*
> *'They be drownded down to hell.'*

In former years, these were hiring fairs and a huge social occasion when families, separated during the year, would come together. It was also the day to buy all those things unavailable locally such as pots and pans, boots and shoes and various items of haberdashery.

Blackberry and Apple Pie

September is also the month for blackberries and the early apple varieties are in season. Blackberry and apple pie was always my favourite childhood dessert. Somerset abounds with blackberries and as children we would be sent out with a collecting tub. Living so close to numerous orchards, sufficient apples and blackberries could be found within $\frac{1}{4}$ mile of my home. Try the following recipe:

> *2 pounds apples, sliced*
> *2 cups blackberries*

1 cup sugar
1 teaspoon ground cinnamon
½ teaspoon ground nutmeg
2 tablespoons flour
1 tablespoon butter
2 rounds of pastry, each 9" diameter

Preheat the oven to 375° F, 192° C, gas mark 5. Mix the apples and blackberries together and blend in the other ingredients except the pastry. Line a pie dish with one round of pastry, add the filling and place the other round of pastry on top, crimping the edges to form a seal. Pierce the upper crust in several places to allow the steam to escape. Bake for about 75 minutes, reducing the temperature if the pastry is browning too quickly. Serve with custard, cream or ice cream.

October

Punkie Night

Across the nation, Hallowe'en is celebrated at the end of October, but at Hinton St George in south Somerset they celebrate their own version called Punkie Night which is held on the last Thursday in October. Local legend tells how the men of Hinton went one night to the nearby fair at Chiselborough and took with them all the lanterns in the village so that they would be able to find their way home. But considerable cider was drunk by the visitors who then enjoyed the company of the young ladies of Chiselborough.

Back at home, the wives and girlfriends became concerned about the late arrival of their menfolk and went off in search of them. With the complete absence of lanterns in the village, all they could do was to hollow out worzel mangolds, a large swede-like vegetable, in the fashion that pumpkins are hollowed out at Hallowe'en. Bearing these vegetable lanterns, they trekked across the hill to the nearby village where their menfolk saw the glowing lights approaching across the hill and, in their drunken stupor, took them to be evil spirits glowing on the hillside. There was an immediate rush to get home, but not by the way they had come where the spirits appeared to block their way. They took the long way home.

The women never let them forget that night. Each year, the young children walk in procession through the village with their punkie lanterns held high, as they sing the punkie song:

It's Punkie Night tonight, it's Punkie Night tonight.
Give us a candle, give us a light, it's Punkie Night tonight.
It's Punkie Night tonight, it's Punkie Night tonight.
Adam and Eve wouldn't believe, it's Punkie Night tonight.

November

Bonfire Night

Bonfire Night on 5th November was the event that triggered the massive spectaculars that have become the Bridgwater and Somerset Carnivals. These carnivals are dealt with in the next section but here we focus on the bonfire tradition. Somerset towns and villages are no different to all the other places across the nation, which hold their local bonfires. Historically, however, Glastonbury could also boast tar barrel rolling down through the High Street and in Bridgwater the huge bonfire in the town centre was constructed with a base of sixty or so empty tar barrels plus a boat or two, all of which were discarded from the nearby docks. Whilst in the north of England there is a tradition for toffee on bonfire night, Cheddar Cheese Straws prove popular with Somerset children.

Cheddar Cheese Straws

> 6 tbsp butter
> 1 cup flour
> 1 cup grated Cheddar cheese
> 1 egg yolk
> 2 tbsp water

Blend the flour and butter to make a fine crumble. Stir in the cheese and then, in a bowl, mix in the egg yolk and water. Stir into the flour mixture and knead until smooth. Place the dough in a sealed plastic container and chill in a refrigerator for at least an hour.

Roll out the dough until it is about ¼ inch thick. Cut into rectangles about ½ inch by 4 inches long. Place these on a lightly floured baking tray and bake for 12 to 15 minutes until they turn a light brown colour. Allow to cool on a wire rack.

As this recipe makes around 70 straws, you may prefer to freeze part of the chilled mixture.

Winter Carnivals

The Friday nearest 6th November brings the spectacular Bridgwater Carnival, the largest illuminated carnival procession anywhere in the world and one of Somerset's best kept secrets. Eighty or so giant floats of 100 feet in length, each portraying a theme and illuminated with up to a megawatt of lighting, process through the streets of this medieval town, the night ending with a massed 'squibbing' display of fireworks which completely fills the town's High Street.

After Bridgwater, the procession, on various nights, moves on to North Petherton, Burnham-on-Sea, Shepton Mallet, Wells, Glastonbury and Weston-super-Mare, each having its own spectacular evening in the carnival calendar.

December

Glastonbury Holy Thorn

In Glastonbury there grows a Holy Thorn, which blossoms at Christmastime. Legend has it that this was brought to Somerset by Joseph of Arimathea, who planted his staff into the ground and from that grew the Holy Thorn. In mid-December each year, a sprig of blossom is cut and sent to the Queen.

Christmas Eve Ashen Faggot

In Dunster, at the Luttrell Arms on Christmas Eve, there is the burning of the Ashen Faggot followed by carol singing. The ashen faggot is a bundle of ash twigs all bound together by withy bands, strips of willow. The faggot is placed onto the

Weston beach huts battered by the winter storms

West Somerset Foxhounds meet at Dunster Castle

large open fireplace and gradually the bands of willow burn through. Each crack, as it sounds to indicate another band of withy has split open, is greeted with a cheer.

Boxing Day Hunts

Despite current legislation, the many hunts across the county enjoy a day's sport on Boxing Day. On the Mendips, Exmoor and the Quantocks, the hounds and their followers can be seen resplendent in their hunting colours. Meanwhile, in Dunster village, Mummers and Morris Dancers perform in the old market place.

QUIZ 2

1. Yoomin vurra gurtzer prize. (Congratulations)
2. Swarm bees ide viyer. (Nice and cosy)
3. If Ida gnawed Ida gonnoam. (I'd rather not be here)
4. Ark a-ee. (Take note of what's said)
5. Ower wheaten-oh? (Don't blame me)
6. A wick zun dee. (Future appointment)
7. Urza gooden, inner. (The lady is well respected)
8. Bis gwain vur jar, den? (An invitation to imbibe)
9. Owvee dun? Avvee dun awright? (An enquiry as to how you have managed with these quizzes)
10. Bleedin' turbull, atcherly. I cassen mek 'ead nur tell ovit. (Your possible response)

Answers at the bottom of the page.

Quiz 2 Answers

1. You're in for a really big surprise.
2. It's warm beside the fire.
3. If I'd known, I'd have gone home.
4. Listen to him.
5. How were we to know?
6. A week Sunday.
7. She's a good one, isn't she.
8. Are you going for a jar, then?
9. How have you done? Have you done all right?
10. Not very well, actually. I am unable to make head or tail of it.

CHAPTER 13

A Tribute to Frederick Elworthy

Frederick Thomas Elworthy lived at Foxdown in Wellington and can justifiably be described as the Word Master of Somerset. He was one of that rare breed for whom the study of dialect held a great fascination and present-day students of dialect are much in his debt. Elworthy died in December 1907, aged 78.

Throughout his life he was a zealous student of folklore and his most important legacy is the work he did in connection with the dialects of West Somerset and East Devon, of which he made a scientific study over many years. In 1876 he produced a study called *West Somerset Patois*, drawing attention to the richness of the western dialect, and *The Dialect of West Somerset* in which he included a detailed list of words, most importantly providing pronunciations. This was in the days long before tape recorders could capture the actual sounds and hence his records are especially valuable to us today.

That publication was followed by *An Outline of the Grammar of the Dialect of West Somerset*, a copy of which sits on my library shelf. It provides a rich selection of common phrases and modes of speech and was described by one of the greatest contemporary philologists (those who study the structure and historical development of languages) as the 'first grammar of an English dialect of any scientific value'.

Its study will reveal just how much of the dialect of the mid 19th century has been lost. Dialect is the spoken word and continually evolves. Hence as it changes, those changes would be lost forever if not documented. The following piece, with translation, is an extract from that publication. It is chosen since it is still comprehensible compared to certain other passages and represents the west Somerset 19th century dialect.

You've ayurd'm tell, annie zur? Bout the cock-craw stowun. Annie shore? Wull, tex true I shore 'ee. An day always do zay thut thickee stowun uvuree toime 'ee d'yur the cock-craw, ee do git up'n turn rown. Zertain, zure! An tiz a turble gurt stowun.

You have heard them tell, have you not, sir, about the cock crow stone? Have you not for sure? Well, it is true I assure you; and they always do say that that stone, every time he do hear the cock crow, he do get up and turn around, for certain sure. And it is a terrible great stone.

An day always considered az to ow der were a pot of money in under'un. An I urd-n awl rown moor'n dree veet deep, an der waz a riggle innun, der waz, an you ken zee un now, an day put a chain rown-un, an eached the plough o' ossez toowun vor to turn'n auver, but daywaud'n able vur to muuv'n, an der ee iz to thiz vury ow-ur.

And they always considered how there was a pot of money under him. And I rid (dug) him all around more than three feet deep, and there was a riddle (groove) in him, there was, and you can see him (the groove) now, and they put a chain around him, and hitched the plough (team) of horses to him for to turn him over, but they were not able for to move him. And there he is to this very hour.

Oh, I tell'ee d'way to go too-un, zur. You knaws the Cat'n Fiddle, dunnee, zur? Wull, durz a paath goose en a leedle vurdur awn, dowun twardz Km Puy'n. Wull, dick der gurt stowen'z up on d'hill, an if you d'vollow dickee path, you'll come too-un.

Oh, I will tell you the way to go to it, sir. You know the Cat and Fiddle, don't you, sir? Well, there's a path which goes in a little further on, down towards Culme Pyne. Well, that great stone is up on that common, and if you follow that path, you will come to it.

Further publications followed in which Elworthy included a complete glossic, a phonetic alphabet devised for scientific expression of speech sounds. His greatest achievement was to be his 900 page *The West Somerset Word Book*, a glossary of dialectical words and phrases. It remains without parallel and is renowned worldwide as an example for other philologists to follow. He also contributed to the *Oxford Dictionary* by collecting 15,000 quotations for its use.

Today very little actually gets written in dialect. That which does is either recorded by language historians such as Elworthy or appears in the form of poetry. Poems can be considered to be the 'fossils' of language, in that the language lives on unchanged from its original form.

Anyone who today wishes to study dialect is faced with the problem that those who can speak strong dialect tone it down when conversing in the presence of people who cannot. The influence of radio and television exposes even the most remote communities to more standard English. It is the country folk of Somerset who are the repositories of dialect and, to benefit from full exposure to that dialect, one really needs to live amongst them.

Most of Elworthy's life was spent in west Somerset. He knew the country folk well and was trusted by them. He was a kind and genial individual who won their hearts and minds and through that in-depth involvement was able to study dialect and produce those great volumes to which I have already referred. What makes his achievement even more remarkable is that, in his time, there were no predecessors to provide a template for such study. It was Elworthy who set the standards for others to follow and in so doing left us perhaps the richest and earliest scientific study of dialect anywhere in the country.

CHAPTER 14

An Insane Somerset Look at British History

Canute Demonstrates His Inability to Turn the Tide – AD 1020

Lady Godiva – 1057

Battle of Hastings – 1066

The death of William Rufus – 1100

The Battle of Agincourt - 1415

Raleigh and the Puddle – 1581

Francis Drake goes bowling – 1588

Charles II and friends hide from the Roundheads – 1651

Nelson at Trafalgar – 1805

Wellington inspects his troops – 1815

The Charge of the Light Brigade – 1854

CHAPTER 15

Zomerset!

Ef you do ax what land is blessed
Wi' works o' natur' o' the best –
I never zeed such 'oodlands yet
Nor vields, so fair as Zomerset.

Ef you do ax where volk do gie
Good cheer an' hospitality –
Zure, better cheer you'll never get
Than in the hwomes o' Zomerset.

Ef you do ax vor sturdy men
Wi' zyve or plough, vor sword or pen –
Goo to the West, vor there, I'll bet,
You'll vind 'em down in Zomerset.

Ef you do ax where comely maids
Be fair as blooths in zunny glades –
What purtier maidens have 'ee met
Than theasemy o' Zomerset?

Ef you do ax where shall I lie
When natur' zaays 'tis time to die –
Oh, come thik day, may forun' let
My bwones be laid in Zomerset.

From *Poems in Dialect* by R.R.C. Gregory; Somerset Folk Press, 1922

*Bob Rogers and Geoff Parsons take a break from haymaking
(John Sparkes)*